D0180937

ASSEMBLING
THE SHEPHERD

..

ASSEMBLING
THE SHEPHERD

Poems by Tessa Rumsey

· ·

The University of Georgia Press

Athens and London

Published by the University of Georgia Press
Athens, Georgia 30602
© 1999 by Tessa Rumsey
All rights reserved
Designed by Betty Palmer McDaniel
Set in 12/13 Centaur by Betty Palmer McDaniel
Printed and bound by McNaughton & Gunn, Inc.
The paper in this book meets the guidelines for
permanence and durability of the Committee on
Production Guidelines for Book Longevity of the
Council on Library Resources.

Printed in the United States of America

03 02 01 00   P 5 4 3 2

Library of Congress Cataloging-in-Publication Data
Rumsey, Tessa, 1970–
Assembling the shepherd : poems / by Tessa Rumsey.
p. cm.
ISBN 0-8203-2168-0 (pbk. : alk. paper)
I. Title.
PS3568.U458A97 1999
811'.54—dc21   99-31497

British Library Cataloging-in-Publication Data available

Thank you Dirty Mike. Thank you David Rumsey & Patricia Jeanrenaud for maps of heaven & earth; James Galvin, for setting the wheel in motion. Thank you Kim Brown, Madeleine & Theodore Jeanrenaud, Max Leach, Thomas Lux, Michael S. Moore, Lisa Palladino, Louis Schwartz, & Brian Young. Grateful acknowledgment is made to the Vermont Studio Center and to the editors & readers of the following journals in which these poems originally appeared: *Black Warrior Review:* "Big Rig the Baroque Sky"; *Colorado Review:* "Diagram for Faith (One monk wrapped)," "Diagram for Faith (We are bound by the sun)," "Diagram for Faith (I took the snow-cast field to mean)," "The Sundial," "Brutalism (Holy city)," "Brutalism (Call me Hollywood)," "Brutalism (Wisteria)," "Wheel (While searching)"; *Denver Quarterly:* "Parable for the Sundial," "The Conference of Birds, or Adornment"; *Fence:* "Corvair"; *Green Mountains Review:* "Poem for the Old Year"; *Phoebe:* "Three Trees for a New World Economy," "Bluebells"; *The New Republic:* "arc projection & mnemonoscope I," "arc projection & mnemonoscope II," "arc projection & mnemonoscope III."

For my parents

The world is everything that is the case.
—*Ludwig Wittgenstein*

CONTENTS

ASSEMBLING
THE SHEPHERD

——————————————

..

PARABLE FOR THE SUNDIAL

OUR CITY BEGINS with a description
of heaven, lushly falls the light along
uppermost tiers of our ziggurat,
smoked and riddled fall the bulleted,
lush along the lowermost tiers. Last night
is spent shells caught in cracks of these cobbled
streets, last night is *Mary, Mary, Mary,*
what rises now is what we cannot live
without. Direction is holy like that,
gregarious and well deranged like that.
A boy keeps a cricket in a matchbox
made of thistles. Thus begin our travels:
resistance. Every independence
is the hush of flowers falling at spring's
end—hands caged around an enlightened head,
and weeping. Outside The Bank accrued two
plastic arms and a leg, spray painted gold.
Devastating, how little they told us
about our lives. We cannot forget them.
The screaming peacocks stitching
our path are the end of this century.
The disassembled walls of the rising
metropolis are the end of this century.
A boy loves his cricket and does not want
to loose it. Whisper "absence." A cathedral
appears around your lips. Yes,
there is an abyss. Yes, we will build
inside it. Try "I don't remember you—"
it will make a strong foundation. The further
we walk away from our city, the more
we carry it with us. From a distance
there is only a glare of gold domes
by which to see—Jerusalem, Mecca,
Benares, Peking, in this story
there is no view from above to meditate,
we never pass the gates

BIG RIG THE BAROQUE SKY

Stand still. Places move within us.
There was the impulse to flee and then there was
New Hampshire, with A, and our refugee vision
of being made more. Connected. Part of
as opposed to dismembered from the nature

program on public television. Once inside
we hoped it would be less of a reunion and more
a realization, *your exile was self-imposed*
or *the door to the garden never closed*
an oiled click would unlock the loamy frame—

in the futuristic city A and I described
a firefly dictatorship. Where meadows
would make us childlike. Beside a cult
of delphinium. Blessed. Following the simple
orientation of the sun. It was our prodigal vision:

forgotten reams of river will embrace us.
Feeling generally cast out, not knowing where
from. We drove in a big rig for days. Over water
of asphalt, Manhattan silver, then white, then
theoretical behind us, and above our big rig

the baroque sky, thickening with decoration
as we spoke of its "sandstone plates" and "Taj Mahal."
At dusk swallows rose over the highway
like black questions of panic, cries—
where will I rest—dip, *will my wings end*

where the wind begins—
rise, do machines dream of spring,
of clouds perplexing their screens?
I objectify what I desire so I can feel
superior and arrived at a maple cathedral,

pledged allegiance to a hierarchy of back roads
and a lilac-green anarchy of light.
At the wet wood shack where syrup was made
A did not cut the wood vein
but he held the blade, beneath custodies

of palmate leaves and long-winged fruits.
We drank straight from the jug. Put our feet
in the river. Decoration disintegrated
as our toes became clear in the water,
what you've been all along

my trigger-finger stroked the channel
changer. And the impulse to flee was a waking
trance state of a sacred order, my Machiavellian
vision: there is no secure mode to possess us
without ruining us, and so the acquisition

turned to loss, say "exiled. And we never even
arrived." Say "dismembered. And the baroque sky,"
say "new principality," say "New Hampshire"
where everything we did was accompanied
by commentary from the leaves—

we can explain back roads and your impulse
to flee in terms of a single substance: water:
the blackest answer: we are never at rest:
and swallows: and factory machines: and
questions: arise

SPHINX: DOCTRINE OF EIGHT NO'S

There is no slit in the scenery through which we may glimpse the gleaming blueprint,
Nor is there a violin in the arms of A Gesture of Greeting to the Rising Sun;
There is no gyroscope *sweet sweet sweet* that can steady the spin of what I'm feeling,
Nor is there any ending;
Nothing is enchanted with itself, but with its reflection of something else;
Nor is the Nile a crystal chapel parroting the Milky Way;
Nothing points to the Imperishable Star transfixing the Luxor in Las Vegas,
Nor does the broken heart oppose existence, beautiful because it is out of balance—

THE SMALLEST EFFECTIVE DISTANCE

Where is the original skin this version can be checked against? Snow,
Cholera, Red Shoe, Nightingale—the image outshines
the actual, the body outshines the soul, the angel
food cake dissolves as you dip it into a cup of black coffee
before me, dark sugar & inevitably, fading. You are my ex & thus
the past must outshine the present in a way that hurts
just to look at. In another country
wasps burrow into October's fallen butter pears
& poppies are halfway drawn toward dying. Everything
in this life has an outline that at sometime will cease
to contain it. So many different renderings of the same wink
& silence that I nearly forgot what time it was—
do you know what lesson this is? Ah, the one where she is made
to decipher desire alone, the one where she wants to be loved
but instead is outshined by her wanting. So easy
to think for a second that the original may soon pale in comparison.
No, says the actual, it was the best you'd ever had, & its one true joy
is that you'll never have it again.

CLEMENTINES, WINTER SOLSTICE, BASHŌ

Dreaming as Galileo dreamed / *awake* but *awash* in the act of looking, planets hanging / ripe fruits on a tree.

If I had a telescope I would train it / to detect the difference / between your true self / your false self, between.

A bowl of oranges and an overturned orange bowl by scanning the borderline / where abundance ends / where abundance begins.

Chinese Orange feather boa hooked to your neck / hooked to the wind / turning away you trailed a horizon behind you.

Moving as a comet moves / *long gone yet still appearing,* insomnia.

Eyelids beat in wingtime, the Green Lion Devours the Sun, sleep comes like a scurrilous lover, *first snow falling.*

On the half-finished bridge.

Appearing as the Medici Stars appeared / your false self first, your true self later / as the four moons of Jupiter.

Captured by the Cloak of Motion a clementine is scrolling / from branch to earth to air to branch to earth—

Stop being. Keep breathing, it's amazing, four years later / and the abandoned vapors / still linger pale among us /

THREE TREES
FOR A NEW WORLD ECONOMY

I

ONCE UPON A TIME we loved the city,
(this might also read *The Vision of X*)
walking beneath bell-sounds, talking beneath
the roaring sound of bees, sun through the trees
made a pale labyrinth (see *dilemmas*)
of shadows to step through. We called the sky-
line (*blue behind*) "black mountain." In winter
expired branches of ice and black quartz
made an aviary for expiring
sparrows (the *tree* represents the *kingdom*)—
those who froze did so among the frozen—
those who rose ate fish among the risen—
(a *pulley-system*) the city was shaped
like a sundial, streets radiating

II

an Angel chilling inside a balsam tree.
She opened her wings (later described as:
I have seen things that you will never see)
and asked me "What kind of tree do I rest
in?" The voluptuous moon shining through
the needles; the dark bars falling upon
her body (a *prison*); she was held
beating inside the black cage (a *vision*)—
one cityscape flat against the horizon;
(*superior* to the previous tree?)
I pointed to it, I said with conviction
(to save the angel with *certainty?*)

"I know that that's a tree" (here
we say X is only *philosophizing*)—

III

crying a little niagara, sending
the children to school with sawed-off shotguns.
In the desert we must say at every
turn: conviction. (Does X think more clearly
in a hot tub or a soup kitchen?)
At the *fin de siècle* the star thistle
signals regeneration. Thus we left
our city (read: *depraved*) for the no-shade
of the joshua (a *veronica*);
we cannot tell our kingdom from a pauper;
the wind around my voice makes a *(phantom)*
aviary; my voice inside the tree
(held beating) blows in no new direction—

THE SUNDIAL

IV

and conceal yourself a little while.
$$\text{They were speaking of a low ceiling, of light}$$
barely shambling in
$$\text{through bullet holes—wondrous were the weapons,}$$
$$\text{bucolic and mad}$$
lay the light against such radiating machines.
$$\text{To measure the colossal metropolis}$$
you must leave it. See *Thickets of the Forest*

V

lie down around the *(riddled)*
$$\text{trunk of a palm tree. We lay down on our sides. We did not}$$
make a shadow.
$$\text{Up above } \textit{le roi soleil} \text{ shimmied its fronds,}$$
$$\text{which fell } \textit{(the gift of tears)}$$
across our sunburned backs, to the east
$$\text{our city shone like superfluous cash,}$$
$$\textit{trompe l'œil}$$
winking YOU WISH, YOU WISH, *(malerisch)*
$$\text{against the vaulted heavens, } \textit{gazebo}$$
against an inked horizon, pimp-kissed,
$$\text{golden, holy ruby bird—}$$
$$\textit{(obscene little ruby}$$
studded bird—)
$$\text{upon which we were looking, vanished into a cemetery}$$

VI

will tell you, though only if you wish it, what I picture to myself
$$\text{when you say } \textit{pleasure.} \text{ I}$$

remember *(what the city tasted like)*

eucalyptus, bougainvillea,

fog the silver green

of eucalyptus, machines half shade, half sun.

In the desert everything is connected by

VII

monochromatic, gold hot, etc.

Dove calls boom-boxed through cold red wires

of dawn, etc., etc.

Where are the *messengers?* and such. Isaiah *(thickets of the forest)*

such and such.

VIII

Chilling among the fragments of *industry,* our desires

IX

as in I am here and you are not, let me count the ways

in which this sucks; loneliness

is time *(buying the body back).* The *citadel*

is a human document. The circumference

of a Byzantine coin is a human document, pressed into

your thinning palm it makes

a simple timepiece, bronze blackens *(to confess)*

when the sun is high above you, you are

a *sundial*—at nones you are the last

(of breaths). Only when put together do my thoughts

become a *shadow.*

Do you know the word

for *hot enough to burn your lips on?* We call

the city Sequence, a.k.a.

(a bed of nails: shining like) A silver virus,

we call the desert

Patience reflected in a smooth white surface, a.k.a Abstinence;
this could be
The Dead Sea scrolling by allegorically;
we are waiting for a *gnomon;* graffiti
on our city flashes more life, more life—
Who is the shadow? *(Who is the light?)*

WHEEL

while searching
for the still point
bodies having floated
downriver
make a clock
in the lake

BRUTALISM

Column B

1. holy city
2. in the day and until evening
3. to approach, to be
4. Remember them for blessing
5. on your name, which is called
6. kingdom to be blessed
7. for the day of war
8. to King Jonathan
9.

BRUTALISM

I

Call me Hollywood.

Imagined sun, bright and black, sometimes appearing over a map we call
our movie set.

One suspicion of crows shellacked to the sky for effect.

Beneath the radar tree M is weeping into a cage of his hands; *I need you to
fly through me;* he cannot find his reflection;

All winter sounds of suffering kept us warm, curled up around a
television.

Overhead, helicoptered versions of wings beating.

Sometimes speaking death, sometimes breathing.

If M sees himself through the gaze of a building; *I have lost the way to my
eyes;* if the building is brutal; *whose lips are these; whose windows;*

(Inside the prison-weather of a radar tree)

Balcony as unrequited love: balcony as hierarchy.

February M stood beneath branches slick with purpled feathers.

Singing *bird, bird, bird,*

To have a bird's-eye view you must have something to look down from.

(Height as angle: height as opulence)

M is shown no hero and a tree full of crows, portrayed as a meadow when
viewed from above.

and were shells of our former selves.

Everything turns into something else then slips away.

M steals figs from his neighbor's tree and whispers.

Forgiveness.

Forgiveness is a wasp at the center of every fig.

2

If M builds an edifice; *I want you to remember;* if the edifice is brutal; *how I saw the bird of paradise;* destroyed from the beginning; *a killing machine;*

No apparent concern for visual amenity—

(Inside the radar tree my body felt like a cage; it was beautiful; turning inside the structure as workers turn inside a factory; windows reflect a face as flowers reflect the sun; *I have become your likeness because—*)

Because a bird of paradise unfolds color into the space between M's body and my body, triumphal arch—

If our materials are obvious;

If a suspicion of crows becomes a black sun above us;

If turning through orange and purple, *I feel my breath inside your lungs, building an empire—*

If I see my eyes through the gaze of another; if I describe what I see;

You will have no peace.

BRUTALISM

Wisteria. Bruised limbs. Tenderness. Such
malfunction of panic salt, of pillar
gun. Machine first. Your met you when shriven.
Sun of made face, my Hollywood, me—

Call

me Hollywood. My face made of sun.
Shriven. When you met your first machine gun.
Pillar of salt, panic of malfunction.
Such tenderness, limbs bruised, wisteria.

TURKISH DELIGHT

I

Under the blue machine of sky they are beginning
to sing a little. Faces turned toward the sun. Changing
direction with each ring of solar gunfire, ending
the silent stratagem. Ending the silent stratagem
once believed instrumental to win signals "from above"—

there is a humming hovering over the deserted field.
Some of us have faith the flotilla is rising
from satellite dishes, our metal sunflowers,
prayers for a deus ex machina to come down to us
with celestial alphabets, scriptural assurances . . .

Will our fallen leader soon return? triumphant?
There was much mythmaking during recent looting
in Mogadishu, the supreme clan-leader portrayed
as turning away, *I was told you were dying,* (interruptions)
from starvation (of pattern) *between two bales*

of hay (awakens intuition), a story begins again
where there is no river, only the static loop
of *rush, rush, rush,* in this region the dead
arise to water their wings with salt and dust.
I have heard a parched pouring *on my forehead*

during the prophetic hours of early morning,
when my eyes are the carmine of failed prayer,
nostalgic for a less confusing past *are letters*
they wait for the violet hour, *to save you,*
for darkness, *and I am always falling away.*

The insomnia maxim reads thus in translation:
"her desire to transcend her design was not
so much an *aspiration* as it was a *reminiscence*
of those forms she once beheld" in factories
where the air was freshened with artificial

hyacinth, to remind the assembly line *tragedy*
begets *obsession* begets *production*, from blood
the sanguine flower grows, forget and suffer
little, or never. "Up there" there is
a morgue of blueprints like a labyrinthine

archive. "Down here" some of us believe
in replication. *The market indulges us*
Johnny Appleseed wires his antenna *until simply*
to a car battery, a sound mixer, a microphone,
getting dressed so no station will escape

his detection *is a complex* with his faith
laid down like a lattice *yet liberating*
challenge of coincidence over landscapes.
The joke goes like this: every dispatch
is a red herring for memory's static loop—

once he broke hyacinth from a stem for me
and I wanted to remind him of hyacinth forever.
"Once" is a diamond bullet splitting open
my forehead with malevolent whisperings
of *lost, lost, lost.* No transmissions

yesterday, watching him turn toward
the station. *She lost her wings.* "If we believe
in the cease-fire," he asked, "will the cease-fire
always exist?" I said "In the desert
there are light bulbs strung up on cacti

but your intuition is enough to see by."
Betrayer. On the platform *repeat never*
we imitated the constructive ambiguity
of overhead broadcasts and kissed
while insisting *over, over, over,*

to keep the airwaves open, we walked,
singing, "There is a great sea looking at me"
and "I would climb thee to see far, far off."
In streets before daylight the masses
on television were flocking to shrines

in the desert *armed with automatic faith.*
A dry mouth remembers ambrosia, and days
generated by nectar, amphibious ship
we build so that we might believe
in a future, carving a code of promises

into the vessel so we might remember
how we once wished to live. Some may
I say love each other from a lack
of faith *repeat never* my satellite
loves the silent rim *beheld the truth*

4

of the sun transmitting messages
to no one, my sun, Dear Sun—
that was me stationed in the deserted
field. I knew you only by a transient
your eyes like riot fires consuming my city

warmth on my head, dispatch of silence
I lived on. After the famine,
drove through the utopic war-torn city
in repossessed police vehicles. Once
every bullet asks "will I ever"

into a body there came a siege

of information to sabotage
the mind's idyllic orchestration.
The revolution reads thus in translation:
and never knows if it has succeeded

interruption. To awaken intuition
I stopped knowing him as "the sun."
Compassless stands the thistle fountain
where there is only the static loop
in the desert, landscape of ghosts

of I and thou—
I will never again say forever—
carved deep, I will not speak—
with a chisel, until spoken to—
carve deeply, until the wood bleeds water,

5

I think I hear a humming, I believe
it is desire thawing pendentives
of perfunctory bodies—were we indolent
or simply praying? I knew a frozen bird,
a frigid wingspan spread inside my chest,

compliments of The Morgue, where the air
was sweetened with hyacinth. Who among us
has smelled the true aroma of hyacinth?
There is a desert of pure feeling
where the wingless water their stumps

with salt, with dust. Their certainty
of impending flight interrupts sand
into river, a story begins again
with desire. In deserted fields
automated priests of faith and industry

transmit fresh alphabets of violet
and fucked-up green into the celestial
machine to spell the blue sky
conquerable. The fate of the uncontainable
reads dominion. The future of the revolution

reads dominion. Divine intervention
speaks thus in translation: *for so long*
I watched you from above, your face a voluble
flower, I thought you'd never speak to me,
I thought you'd wither first and fade—

DIAGRAM FOR FAITH

I took the snow-cast field to mean everything golden spends a season dark and drunk and dried-up under the lethal machinations of languid angels, to be biting the curb and have your head kicked in under the most beautiful sun in the world means brightness, means every color explodes while somewhere, frozen, a dark stallion stands epic on a snowy field. I walked into one and was told the other. Nevada, November. The locomotive's baroque locutions inched across the desert, which I took to mean everything sleeping dreams of industry, to be bleeding and broken on the sidewalk while above you ambrosial clouds evolve means loneliness, means the world continues though your faith has ceased—and warm clouds of breath release, from the stallion, somewhere, in a cold field, frozen. I frightened one and was terrified by the other. Los Angeles, November. I took the urban myth to mean everything moving flies through uncertainty, to be at the receiving end of a dream that begins, in someone's heart, years before, and travels through countless cells and seasons until it is transferred angrily from a foot to your temple means progress, means every temple is as holy as the spirit that destroys it. All around the wild horse the world is shaking, is releasing. I did not see the beast until it stood before me, still breathing.

SPHINX: THE SOUL AS GUIDE,
SHOWING THE WAY

Fear of the future can cause a Pharaoh to enlist a ladder into his burial chamber, can impel

a boyfriend to kick in a door on Epiphany. The cold planet spinning

at the end of the universe was said to have inspired annihilating powers when discovered,

was said to have spurred the splitting of the atom. A voice whispers *imagine me.*

Today I will open a wood plank with a hole in it, which begs the question *what kind of tree do I rest in?* of entrance, of a lone body passing its threshold. Linen napkin

pulled through a ring, *nothing hidden up my sleeve,* shards of mahogany and white paint portraying

a solar system on the Egyptian rug, first we dreamed of rain, next we created the flood—

RADAR RANCH RECONNAISSANCE

Jessamine. Umber. Honeybee. 580 nanometers of radiant energy, sunflower, lion colored, in the reconnaissance the air is yellow and lemon-scented. A girandole,

one of the basic human requirements is the need to dwell, however temporally,

inside the deserted orchard of granulose bark. Radiate sympathetic branches, and I will inhabit the sound, limonite, ochre, uranium ore shelter,

with a place on the planet that belongs to us, and to which we belong,

in part he was sympathetic to my childhood when he colored the orchard umber. To learn me a lion, a sunflower, a marmalade of inhabitable yellow,

this is not, especially in the tumultuous present, an easy act,

imparting a radiating sunflower into my childhood. He built a lemon girandole inside me, a sympathetic nevada. To reflect him. He learned to build branches.

As attested by the uninhabitable no-places in cities everywhere,

incongruous were the plates of earth he photographed, as I saw, and heard, and bore witness, over the collage he later created, a girandole of colors,

we require help, allies in habitation, to connect ourselves, we have at hand

in yellow: marmalade, the sky: yellow, the sky: marmalade as he built it, plate by plate, creating witness of incongruous earth as he saw and heard

many allies, if only we call on them, other upright objects—stand in for us.

Increasingly we began to reflect each other: the orchard: the incongruous earth: my childhood: the collage he later created: the ranch he found near winnemucca

in sympathetic imitation of our own upright stance, to serve as the testimonial

indented into the mountain. A concrete radar station. Abandoned, reflecting
the desert in its windows as I saw through them, as he photographed lemons

of our own care, and breezes loosely captured can connect us with the infinite,

inside the abandoned radar station. He built an umber-colored girandole and in
the collage he later created the girandole was reflected inside me. Radiating—

"The sun never knew how wonderful it was until it fell on the wall of a building"

increatly, and in this uninhabitable no-place I build, plate
by incongruous plate, an alleged ranch of sympathetic branches, an orchard

of jessamine, lemon-scented, built for me once before, that I might bear witness.

THE STRANGER

And / Because I mistook the rising
Moon for a burning metropolis,

Atomic against the spider horizon
Because the air was mellifluous.

With dragonflies, because to begin again
I had to die / And split

Like a sacred ox under the monk's holy
Axe—cyan

Coins of dusk rushed through my chest
As I fell to the east / As I fell to the west

City of burning shepherds across the desert
A flock of phantom smoke took flight

My eyes black maps / As the light
Shone through me. A body broken

May pray to begin again / Let me please
Begin again. The sun was drunk

And stumbling. There was a hawk
Whose wings had been torn off

Inside my chest. Something deep
Was dying, fighting for a last and a last

Breath. Death ripened on the orchard's
Ashen branches, corseted tight with bees

I found the warped coyote wired
Between two deranged apple trees

Skinned, shimmering, guts swinging
Like delicate pendulums built to measure

The earth's dark minutes (pain peeling
In ticks off the sweet barbed rack)

I looked for the hunter hidden. For wings
Strapped to a bloody back. One eye

Questions the world from inside
A human cage. The other belongs

To someone who has been suffering.
Each treat the other as a stranger—

Right hand slits coyote's throat / Left
Hand caresses his shoulder, shudder

The blade between two halves of one
Truth—I wept for the coyote.

I pulled the wire tighter.

NEVER MOROCCO

I

The limits of our language are the limits
of our world coo-cooeth the philosopher
into my love's tin ear (Tangier? But I was nowhere

near Morocco—) as he sucks a luminous
alphabet of smoke from the crack pipe,
as the alley weather turns from inadequate

to oceanic, as the picture is bamboozled
toward a more tented-Saharan-tea-party-
meets-nomadic-American-junkie motif—

to his east, neon Casbah blinks pistachio
and shocking pink, camels ache aimlessly
along the duned horizon, Where oh where

is my orange tree? my *casablanca?* In ruins—
here, he ignites—hermaphrodite
city folds in upon itself, spelling

swarms of retarded bees gone ritalin
among his inner trees *you are not what*
you say you are not what you say you are not—

II

You could be barefoot and heroic, addicted
to chain guns and rocket launchers
and still the desert would not need you

funny to be dying for the mirage's
deranged marriage of distance
and liquid and realize everything

you've ever uttered is the projection
of a picture—*sea of sand, flying
camel, sandstorm, Bedouin*—you

are not where you say you are, epileptic
beneath the city's dank and fogbanked
dawn, the book will kill the minaret

the alphabet will kill the icon, what
did the philosopher say that night,
beneath the never and the phantom

orange trees (pornography for the bindles,
rubberbands for the bucks?)—whisper *lover
dying* whisper again *not breathing*

III

And what is a "tree"? And what is "seeing"?

DIAGRAM FOR FAITH

One monk wrapped in cloth the color of a fashionable nuclear sunset
is coming undone upon the subway platform, a saffron-tinted Shiva
working myriad limbs around the rush hour of eternal *return* of eternal
renounce, as if multiplicity were the answer to ambivalence, as if
a wheel's point of stillness hinged upon its spokes' psychotic dance—
crowd chants. Monk rewinds his habit. One minute you are in love
and Faith is as intrinsic to the landscape as Money and Death, clock
behind the season, reason behind—the reason you hold on too tightly
is the reason everyone leaves you. *Boom* the train doors slide shut, thus
the wheel turns, thus the wheel turns, inside that station's tiled blueprint
you wait for a fata morgana or his blue hair to materialize out of evening
editions wilted condoms hypodermics, believing that if you stare
hard enough at unrelated objects a pattern will reveal itself,
mandala, microcosm, bird's-eye-view, meaning
a mirage still moves you, meaning every lover should come
with a sign: WARNING: CAPE DOES NOT ENABLE USER TO FLY—
being abandoned by your lover may lead to raptor delusions
and/or methedrine hangovers, as you tear the wings from a hawk;
you tear the arms from your torso; bloody back, deranged
instruction manual, *how will I know what's true?* You use
your search engine to look for "shit" and then "Aquinas"; despite this
there is still no equation to make him appear in the station
where an underground hurricane of speed, superconductors, and cerulean
space unravels a holy man's diagram for faith—

THE WAR

I saw the sun get random and bust out
into a streaming glass necklace he said I waved my revolver
in the air like a glory torch it spelled *entanglement*
the slow drawl of the *g* getting ass-fucked by the *ment*
then fading like an extinct color into the ether
some nights you can just fuckin' *feel* Darwin
gettin' busy all over your freaked-out word—I mean
world—I was wrapped in dying
star breath I was breathing
out star scriptures and this, he said, was after
the Dextromethorphan Hydrobromide Romilar Brown Elixir
a.k.a. cough syrup wore off. I shot the Jap in the face.
Fucker was grinning at the fireworks and each tooth
in his oyster mouth was bigger than Jesus
and all the billboard planets advertising heaven have you ever
been sleeping in a clearing and heard the moon
getting sliced by the wings of a helicopter
something like something resembling the citrus smell
of lilac in an alley and the selfishness of bees
slurred mechanical speech
of reluctant steel angels
have you ever been sleeping in a clearing and heard the moon bleed
in sparkling archipelagos of light have you ever
woken from dreams of redemption
woken to find that you are bleeding beneath
a heaven that will never let you in—
that night beneath the fireworks and steel interruptions
I saw God burst
I heard the most beautiful road it wrote
you will never reach the end
you will walk until your feet become roots and your roots become ground
your breath will walk beside you until it becomes the sound
of suffering. If two make peace
then what is one man
with his dream of progress

chopping up the moon like a kung-fu Elvis—
I shot his face. I heard
our road explode.
Go, said the entanglement. Go
and wash your bowl.

MAN-TORPEDO-BOAT

If he had loved me he would not have designed
the land mine the land mine
that jumps up from black matted soil
to the level of a heart the land mine
that explodes while floating in the air
like an iron cherub like the blameless conjunction
between *man* and *killing machine*

If he had loved me he would not have written
the executioner's list for Tuesday the list
spotted with jam and breadcrumbs and the hubris
of early morning coffee
tucked away into the trousers of a messenger
holding one end of a rope the rope tied
to the last name on the list

If he had truly loved me he could not have delivered
the letter bomb the letter bomb
wrapped in luminous paper of onion skin bejeweled
by the riddling stamps of Egypt the letter bomb
addressed in the goldblack songlines of Arabic and pushed
through the mailslot like the suggestion of new love
and its necessary language

If he loved me like bread and water like air like thinking
he would have reinvented his speech
like the poet Marinetti in Italy
on the eve
of World War I
searching for a new grammar
to capture the velocity of the machine gun

Every noun should have its double
that is
the noun should be followed

with no conjunction
by the noun
to which it is related
by analogy

Man-torpedo-boat.
Darling-land mine-heart.
Hand-list-executioner.
Messenger-rope-prisoner.
Letter bomb-mailslot-last breath.
Lover-machine gun-corpse.
Corpse-lover-me.

YOUR DIAMOND SUTRA

What was it we used to sing to make certain we got through this? Your broken
gun and the automatic heart introduced early in the story
suggest volcanic williwaws of operatic hoo-rah, songs
originally envisioned by a sallow musician drowned in ruffles
and velvet neophilia, *I'm losing you, I'm losing you, I'm* no music
yesterday, walking alone along the Interstate. The diamond city
fissured toward the bay, the way an ersatz flower
sparkles, then slowly fades, at precisely the speed the color the cadence
it was programmed to. When I dream of you
the end has not yet begun / is endlessly beginning.
Black sky automaton illuminated by the slow burn of dying
stars, soundtrack of terror we sleep by. We sleep
and elsewhere the song to describe our dreaming
is spun on a soundtable, a thumb harp, a xylophone.
I woke, and the memory of such melodies sent me mute
and searching. Drowned in flowers. Such ersatz
neophilia. The fatalistic city sparkled toward the bay,
the way a machine built for dying blossoms, then quickly
fades, at precisely the speed the color the cadence
it was programmed to. When I dream of you
scratch—I dream of you, I dream of losing you
which has or has not yet happened, depending on the sutra
we are currently inhabiting, depending on the pop song
playing on the lone transistor radio. The algorithmic city
unfolded in diamonds toward the bay, the way
an orchid builds itself, then methodically fades,
at precisely the speed the color the cadence
it was programmed to. I'm losing you. Somewhere
in a previous and velvet century a musician
(drowned in *flowers?*—drowned in ersatz neophilia)
plays music to describe this dreaming, not yet
begun—not ending—yet endlessly beginning.

MAP OF TIBET

In other words *globe held against the slow*

revolution of a Xerox machine *revolution*

of time hands harboring one planet's design

upon a dark pond of glass *the sun blasts*

now fifty years have passed *and the light*

spills out of collecting maps backed on

linen or an occasional *living inside a panther*

and a prayer bead simultaneously morocco

leather cover he lifts each portrait *every*

one has a monastery to which he belongs

of mountain of island of riverbed onto

the evolution machine—*here is the owner*

and here is a paper photo of his fingers

around all of China, captured on copper

c. 1731 *in ruins* before his sun had begun

then pressed into plaster and painted

every thing he offers does not really exist

for instance blue is the desert

lilac the deepest sea here is his birthplace

and here his unknown country—paper copy

of his fingers and a globe *every step taken*

gives a footprint to the stone with a hole

inside China he cannot know where *his music*

is beginning nor when his country ends—slow

slow revolution of breath crusading over lips—

then globe—then hands—a map is for those

who cannot see the land—*where do I belong*

is the song of light spilling out

of a mechanical sun as he remembers

the way one *building a monastery* before him

saw this world as an order to be chosen—

and in the morning his ground is frozen

CORVAIR

As if your true self were shrouded in inaudible fog: the will
to speak is often absolved by the sheer inability to enunciate
the simplest of questions: *where is your heaven?* And *why
did you leave me?* What was the meaning of that hypnopompic
driving expedition, the car like a body whose heart was a wheel,

you thought you could steal minutes from the timeline
by driving faster, velvet Monza ether, soft top down, stars
performing their star roles though *death* is often mistaken
for *tireless dreaming*, what is the meaning of the true self
speechless, yet desperately steering the body whose heart:

on autopilot: inaudibly searches for new ways to be alone

THE NAPOLEON HOUSE
(A HISTORY AND GEOGRAPHY)

It was a *conseil du lion*, a plan devised to build troops into the town
to erect blockhouses, barracks, fortifications, fire cannon continuously

while I defied my assignment and drove south through Missouri until
hidden purple in the field Arkansas was revealed, an accusatory finger

to kill as many horses as possible and then salt the meat, appropriate
grain, appropriate sugar beets, winter silently there until spring

reprimanded the withered landscape, a purple tree in Tennessee outside
my station wagon, I followed a road concurrent with historic waters

to fight through the enemy, into secretive purple regenerating the field
after serving a sentence to winter obediently, the well frozen white,

I stuttered the name of the river recurring Louisiana, missing the turn-
off, missing someone I left confined in the futuristic town behind me,

paralyzed, the cold a confining orchestration, huddled on wet stones
patriotically despite the shock of warm blood beneath blue skin, despite

frozen and asleep, wandering through purple, as I through purple, awake,
as I engulfed into repeating swamp, ambushed, into the springtime of

teeth grinding, fever, asphyxiation, arms unable to hold the cold away,
learning to sleep under the lunette, the tin roof, the ravelin, dreaming

New Orleans, into a bar built by expatriate Frenchmen who sipped absinthe
in steamy cafes hatching vaporous plots to rescue Napoleon, I am reading

of regeneration, climbing from stuttering bodies to touch besieged fields
with accusatory fingers until a purple-green-gold, a lemon-fuchsia recurred

and bourbon is continuously delivered, a beautiful balcony, affording
a view of a river I do not recognize, unfamiliar orchestration, I wander

over Napoleon sleeping, defy the plan of the lion, learn to slip through
the ravelin, then beyond stuttering water, and over, the enemy

CLEMENTINES, WINTER SOLSTICE, IKKYU

Every day / is a dark cave / the satellite passes undetected / undetected the satellite passes / dark days / insomnia cave

Priests minutely examine the Dharma / and endlessly chant complicated sutras / my noctambulist steers a burning Nova

Across the metropolized horizon / searching for his lost Sun / till he becomes The Bright One / bedizening a black harbor

With his Chevy's highbeamed chiaroscuro / imitating that which is most desired / the Dharma / the complicated lover

Imitating what is most desired / so that one moment in the future / the rock will become the river / a car seduced

By the force majeure of its driver / and we are all verging on machine anthropomorphism / the priests curl into ink

Into corporeal sutras / slumber comes like a spurious lover / the Sun falls asleep in an orange

Ripening at dawn / a mnemonic device / under the purple sky's bone chignon—

You were prepared to be the light by which the object of desire found its true color / not the first / but the hidden

Second light of the Sun / your future self orbiting each dark day / yet passing endlessly / undetected

SPHINX: INSTRUCTION MANUAL

Dominion Despite Disaster.
Chant it like a mantra.
Weld copper kettles and steel pots to your biceps and thighs.
Design yourself into a gleaming temple transmitting messages to no one.
Wonder if this is a test.
Mark the days on a gourd tree.
Eat beetles, shit in a hole.
Wait for a celestial hand to touch you softly and turn your kingdom to gold.

YOUR DIAMOND SUTRA

After the gun was held to my head, "the gun was held to my head"
became the music I lived by, schadenfreude we walked to.
A sixteen-year-old staring down the barrel of a revolver
may be said to resemble a sunflower, may be said to resemble
the space between two magnets drawn irrevocably to each other.
Cool blued steel playing against her temple, pop song exploding
from the lone transistor radio. Broken and shaking in the broomcloset
all she could do was sing. To celebrate the victory of Melody,
king of demons, over Violence, goddess of prosperity, the way
is lit by many candles so all may see the path they walk on—

BLUEBELLS

By early light a hand blesses the outdoor mall with two bombs
tucked into litter bins, ticking, ready to blossom. It's spring.
One minute between blasts will determine who lives and who dies,

seconds ripe with choices: which way to run? towards the church?
or into the thicket? to kneel over the bleeding mother by the torn
bench? to reach for the tree branch? seconds? time no longer?—

traveling in a blue sirocco my view of England is terrorized
by wind and speed over time. My stepfather accelerates religiously.
I would like to capture the celebrated nuclear power plant in color

with my Polaroid. The moment before the triple tower's smoke spills
over—position and frame the picture, as smoke, press red button,
seizures, machine offers photograph with the first commandment,

renders a second in tones recognizable. Outside the window
historical landmark and Burger King transmute into a single
vision repeating with kaleidoscopic variety. Medieval castle blurs

with Roman fort and Viking ship. Cathedral develops shopping
center that is overpopulated and filling with voices, sunlight.
Picnicking by the river we wonder why we feel sedated. At night

we dream of machines in a voyeuristic, valiumed sleep, of the enemy
hiding in the television. Ticking. A pitcher tipped and frozen just before
epileptic water pours over, perched the warbling sparrow, suspended

on the thinnest branch, of revelation. As beak opens bombs call to black
crops. There shall be awaken. Time captured. No longer. Liberated
on the riverbank we ask how to preserve and rewind the film,

who is allowed to sip the Irish whiskey, how to listen to radio news
while eating lunch. How to leave the river the way we found it,
the way it first appeared to our hungry eyes: hysterical and alive.

One minute to decide. Sunlight seizes the metal roof of the river,
the watery sidewalk. Voices in the crowd. A movement. A bystander
explodes, inside my brother's laughter, into springtime, I hand

my sister the ripest pear and shrapnel rips a girl's ankle to forsythia—
the daffodils are amazing, so yellow, spilling, screaming boy's leg
is caught in the river and a hole in the spiral widens, widens,

my stepfather the bystander under Ash trees, under
warm weather, under the overhead music, under winter
and spring simultaneously, superimposed on the fading photo—

There shall be time no longer. The recurring phrase. To harmonize
histories into concurrent voices, into a single movement of exploding
sedated crops. There was so little time to decide where to run.

And the fugue of voices left me by the proverbial river. My foot caught
in the wide spiral. The dialectic was drowned by hysterical waters.
Time, epileptic, spilled. The black shoots ripened. Into a field. Of bluebells.

TULIP TRIPTYCH AND ETHNIC CLEANSING

One. Infinite delay. Second crying answers
Lay your dead field down in opulence
Years ago black crows invaded our country

Lay your dead field down in red. Money
To form a vast expanse of mosaicked flowers
Over existing architecture, coated in honey

And shone, and could not erase, and
To form a vast expanse of mosaicked flowers
Let's say one tulip bulb

From Turkey embedded in beeswax,
Let's say "crack" in the older sense of "best"
All winter on hands and knees below windmills

Workers warming frozen stems with breath
Five cents an hour so spring might exist
As architecture, coated in money

He said *black crows* he said *our country*
He pointed straight at——
And shone. And could not erase. And

It was as if each had been placed exactly
Where it was. A tense machine
In a tight green uniform of Spring——

Running through city streets on crack
Thus the field was opulent——
Screaming *you* ARE *me* at bystanders

They were wired to the architecture
It was as if each had been placed exactly
At arm's length. Let's say one arm's length

Between electrocuted tulips, let's say
"Crack" in the newer sense of "fascism"
Ubiquitous rush of a field in full flower

He said *black crows are invading our country*—
One. Infinite delay. Second crying answers
He pointed straight at me

DIAGRAM FOR FAITH

We are bound by the sun.
Beneath the gamelan's dull rain.
The phantasmagoria delivers its story.
I want to warn you.
Against me.
The sun destroys all flowers.
Drinking coffee in tin cups, banging the bronze metallophones.
Inside that island's cryptic station.
Smoke smoke and watch the monkey dance.
Every face in the audience a burning poppy.
Field of flowers aflame, and above us, the lunatic stage.
Play my spine, eat some poppies, make yourself epic.
You want to warn me.
Against you.
"At that moment I knew how afraid—"
Behind the screen.
Shadows behind shadows puppets behind.
Puppets the blue flames behind the blue flames the *dalang* jerking.
The arms the legs behind the *dalang* the dull rain.
Of the gamelan, elephantine, showgirl, sunshine.
Bright currents burning between us, breaking open.
The bamboo xylophones.
Transfixed by shadows.
"I had become" bound to the sun.
And burning, behind you.

WHEEL

You don't decide to become destroyed—
                         it just happens.
                                          Of our future collecting
as exploded apples recollect, into a meadow
                              of bodies spilling
                                            across a battlefield
symphonically, of sandalwood, of ashwood
                              (who once wept as he fell into the field
of a bullet) of beaches
                   lit by burning palm trees and aeroplanes
                                           lit by fires below,
of suffering—
            not yet—
                 of my stepmother playing cello
                              after a death (there will be a storm
of fingers, of notes
                  across my chest) of weeping grasses
                                  she will hear a music of bullets
and builds a field inside my ear,
                   a flaming branch
                            of sky, what we will see reflected
as what we once predicted, road
                 made of sand
                        whose route the wind erased—
                                            not yet—
Our future will recollect
                 all suffering. City whose storm takes shape
                                  as we approach it,
may we walk these streets of burning
                   breaths falling, and if you cannot find me listen
to sandalwood. Of ashwood
                 she will hold the cello and decipher a soldier
                                      built of apples.

Here is our future. Of suffering

       not yet—

               please recollect

                         nothing. I knew not where

this music is beginning. Your voice

              burns through the battlefield

                         weeping wings against

my body. This storm is a wheel. We will be stilled

                  not by design

                       but by acceleration,

into fields, of freesia

        it became destroyed—

               and then it happened

ASSEMBLING MY SHEPHERD

Thrown out of a third story window on acid late spring.
And I put my hand to his forehead to say: listen. Be still.
I am here. Sitting calmly on the sidewalk breathing glass
stuck to his broken body, transformed by sudden flight
so I held him. And was an unseen protector in the rarefied
atmosphere of an unsteady city. I get scared. I get

terrified and really it was my mother standing over him
as I watched from curtained windows—
how she wrapped him in a blanket. How she said: breathe.
How I sequenced my arms around my torso and saw
him coming through a crack in the window to take me with him,
she was all that stood between us, I built her a village

and hid behind the cistern when weather came, and when
I was a worm there was sun, and when I was a lion, sun,
her land had a quality of time that steadied me under the sun.
I get scared. I get so you slip in through a crack seeing I
saw your face, you had to be feared before you could be loved,
my mother held my shoulders and said *you are a shepherd,*

the village, torn down, I listen for your instructions

ASSEMBLING MY SHEPHERD

Inside lilac your lungs, a castle of lilac breathing.
        Once an alley-lined-lilac mother said,
And you adored it at this point in your personal history,

Then the yellow school bus broke down and the driver
        Was stabbed to death as you were
dropped off, into the purple of April, he had been hiding

Under the back seat waiting for you to transgress
        And then she stopped breathing, lilac,
yellow, breathing, disappearing, and the king of glory

Shall wedge himself under the surface and wait until
        You are not watching, until the last
Two feet dangling have passed down a metal aisle,

You stepped into the lilac-lined alley as the yellow bus
        Pulled away, the driver, destroyed,
And I remember a thick smell of flowers filled my lungs

Like castles, never to be the same again, as he removed
        Himself from under the back seat
And into the open, stabbing the driver then retreating,

Purple saturation breathing, who will show us where
        the enemy hides, under veils—
I was never, life of lilac, terrified, until spring.

ASSEMBLING MY SHEPHERD

I lay a nickel face-up on tracks
at dusk and sit by the river
scrolling, discovering the way again
and again, I fall in love
with you in a city every spring,
when you leave everything
seems erased utterly and the reason
I remember is love, and the way
I forget is love, love
learning the same direction
differently each time
I come to tracks at dawn
where features have been erased.

WHEEL

We may rise. In the west
a deafening harbor of no-
water. Drive beside
the dried-up river whore
and weep for what you have
not given

POEM FOR THE OLD YEAR

January. The archer aims at himself.
His target is the eye of a fish. River
is frozen. Field rises in mists of lost
desire and steams the sealed sky open.
Fish be ruby-weeping. Fish be nailed
through scale onto door of silver birch.
Over the mountain beaten boy searches
for his teeth inside a clump of brambles.
The sound of thorns through his skin
is *mercy.* The sound of a beautiful fish
being nailed to a door is *mercy, mercy.*
Nobody knows the origin of music,
or who wind pitches for between rock
and rock like a bronco heart kicking
in its cage. Breeze seduces bow. Bow
abandons arrow. Boy finds shelter
in thicket and hears music of his breath
through ugly, twisted thistles. Come
home. It's time to begin again. A boy
is nailed to the door and a fish is aimed
at an archer, mountain is weeping rubies
onto frozen river while wind grinds
two new teeth. Who are you
inside the music of another's suffering?
When I was a nail I loved only
the hammer. When I was a breeze I died
on a door. When I was a fish
I swam without knowing not yet, or last
breath, or shore.

CLEMENTINES, WINTER SOLSTICE, BUSON

The long night / the journey come full circle / the woman sleeping in the park / wrapped in boas of tinsel.

Inside the boudoir's peachy borders a bowl of oranges shines in technicolor blah-blah / *clementines*, darling.

Call them *clementines* / a constellation of perfect obedience, always seedless, yet rarely eaten / she is dreaming.

The earth is careening / impeccably within its allocated system / we say there is an order to everything / but we mean.

Subservience / *Coolness—the sound of the bell as it leaves the bell*

Would you like an orange from China? / *pouf pouf* / angry sun plucked from a tree in Szechwan, hustled through India.

Carted across Arabia, barely bruised on its evolution to the New World—as the fruit passed westward / so did the word.

As the sun rose / I chose to see again / shining in her crystal peignoir, curled beneath the damp / the flaming eucalyptus.

Curled beneath the flaming eucalyptus / twinkled an exploded view of the cosmos / we weep so that we may cease.

To bear witness / orange offered as a symbol of condolence / of the journey / come full circle / and the long night—

YOUR DIAMOND SUTRA

Once the mirage was endless—once the horizon was distant—once you arrived
On the landscape and believed that without you the landscape would cease to exist
The road is wide, straight, bright, crystal, and the sun is at the end of it—out
Of you, out of tune, radio moon transmitting winter to the naked maples outlined
In snow, cold bandages for the abandoned, pale attempts to fill the hole—
Rowboat suspended above the blank meadow—*you passed through the cathedral,*
your soul was carried by sparrows—halo held up by air, field of rusting poppies
But no stems appear, horse without a rider, breath without—lost world shimmering,
A pot full of copper pennies—*pressing close to you, as if you were cold, flying over*
The snow—one radiant coin placed upon each believer's tongue—*what is the body,*
What have I done—dying to remember—your eyes in December—blue fish frozen
Inside such white and frozen ponds—*where does the body go, where have you gone*—
(Later, in the death field, such black and poppy horses—) how will I find you
When I become the dust?—*but the sun*—the sun—*the sun is at the end of us.*

All right; a man is afraid of his wife. What then?
Often behind them, a tiny golden city hovering
like a hand-held mirage, its stoic towers suggesting
an equation for reaching heaven, sky blue unfolding
like a book inside whose pages it's been written
the proof is too long to include in these margins—
Outside the city walls, a winged bombilation
of birds portrayed in precious metals and crimson
to signify something remarkable has happened.
If we could persuade the birds to rebel against
their roles within the holy city's allocated system
then perhaps I could point to the floating apparition
as an explanation of time, and the inevitability
of losing you. Watch—without the fanfare of fangled
feathers and whirling flocks the city simply
founders—gray, static, unreadable. In other texts
and phantom cities love is portrayed as a fact
to believe in: *a parrot would not do more for an almond.*
After incalculable hours of desert sojourns and nights
spent breezing inside the date palm, our delinquent
local avis find paradise in the surface of an oasis.
I watch your face forever. sic. *I bob my head as you do.*
If Fear is Recognition in sly disguise then Knowing
is a kind of Praying, *I have always loved*
you; I have become you; and behind me, a tiny
golden city, whose sleeping King awakens
to silence and is certain that what once declared
his kingdom holy has now retreated from the sun.

ARC PROJECTION & MNEMONOSCOPE I

Collapsing stars / declarations of betrayal *so dense no light escaped.*
Barn music at midnight, lone transistor radio launches its messenger.
To the four moons of Jupiter: transcriptions of abundance in winter.
Let down and hanging around, you know I'd never leave you.
Soul transmits to body above the subterranean spacesick alien.
Earth's cold apples drawn, quartered, and fed to hysterical horses.
Saddle slung over the frozen rope swing, *loneliness rides toward me.*
In one fell swoop the sky was saved for our inspection and amazement.
Appaloosa against the unbridled snow, a lone transistor radio.
Landlocked and blue, *one day I will grow wings, and leave you.*

Feeding the steaming beast a sugarcube, I think of you.
Not ordered but not resembling any flower or riot formation.
"If the rock were a diamond, the simple act of pointing—"
Would mean wanting: barn music, wild poppies, mob logic.
The night we kissed, your eyes unfastened beneath the bodacious.
Luna and locked lips—four years later, looking frozen in the river.
Two blue fish; not chaotic; but not resembling any diamond.
Or rock formation, which would mean creating, in order.
To exist, I feed the sugarbeast, warm the water, unfreeze the fish—
Your river's cold choplogic seduces, then reduces, my hot dry heart.

ARC PROJECTION & MNEMONOSCOPE III

Wanting the old love, lost way, unsolvable sky, we fold back.
Into its pale cocoon a twisting butterfly, baroque wings beating.
Incessantly against the undivided snow: a buzzing detuned radio.
Frozen without you and feeling so low, blue body transmits to soul.
Praying to the four moons of Jupiter: send eternal loops of winter.
An alien thing landed upon our shore, making us mute, making us more.
Endless and afraid: arc projection between the barn and the astrolabe.
Connecting "my snow mnemonic field" with "your blue celestial city."
Butterfly fold unfurling to infinity—*Go on your strange journey.*
Rise up out of the old beast, launching arrows into the riddled heavens.

THE CONTEMPORARY POETRY SERIES

Edited by Paul Zimmer

THE CONTEMPORARY POETRY SERIES

Edited by Bin Ramke